FARE Anxiety

7 Quick & Simple steps to rid yourself of anxiety!

Dr Marcia Becherel, MD, Ph.D
&
Dr Olivier J. Becherel, Ph.D

Joshua Books
JoshuaBooks.com

HEALTH & WELLBEING

All correspondence to the publisher
Joshua Books
PO Box 1668
Buddina 4575
Queensland Australia

First Printed 2009

ISBN 978 0 9805338 4 2

Category: Health and Healing: Author: Title

Joshua Books
JoshuaBooks.com
HEALTH & WELLBEING

Praisings

"Truly a great book to help you break free from the self-imposed prisons of anxiety we often create ourselves."

Angelo Mera, Ph. D,
Trainer of NLP, Time Line Therapy™ and Hypnosis.

"This Book is a must read on my students reading list and is a must read for anyone who is a student of life that wants to understand, master, and say farewell to anxiety."

Teresa Ryan
Worldwide Trainer of NLP, Time Line Therapy™
Hypnosis, and Coaching.

"A concise, practical and easy to understand book on anxiety. Even if you don't do all the exercises, you will find some quotes and/or paragraphs that "stand out" for you. Write this down and keep them with you. They will serve you well."

Sue Gale
Master Practitioner of NLP,
Time Line Therapy™ and Hypnosis.

DISCLAIMER:

The authors of this book do not dispense medical advice or prescribe the use of any technique as a form of treatment for physical, medical or psychological problems without the advice of a physician, therapist, or psychologist either directly or indirectly. If you are currently being treated by a physician, psychologist or other healthcare practitioner for any condition or disease, consult with that provider prior to changing or modifying any treatment program. The intent of the authors is only to offer educational and transformational information to help in your quest for emotional freedom and spiritual wellbeing. In the event you use any of the information and techniques described in this book for yourself, the authors and the publisher assume no responsibility and liability for your actions.

Time Line Therapy™ is a registered trademark of Tad James, licensed exclusively to the Time Line Therapy™ Association, Inc.

Drs. Marcia & Olivier J. Becherel are both members of the Time Line Therapy™ Association, Inc.

Anxiety
Stress
Happiness
Joy
Which one
do I Want?
FOCUS
E
Emi

Dedication

To my parents for giving me the great gift of life
and for their Wisdom & Unconditional Love.

To my husband, Olivier,
for sharing an amazing and inspired life with me.

Marcia

To my parents, Francine & Jacky, for the Great Gift of Life,
their Unconditional Love & Trust, and to my wife, Marcia,
for sharing it with me.

To the Implicate Order of the Universe for letting it unfold ...

Olivier

Acknowledgements

Farewell to Anxiety is the result of our journey for a permanent personal development and growth, and the encounter with many friends and teachers. Writing is always a collective effort and many people have contributed to the production of this book in various ways.

It is not possible to name them all, however let us mention a few of them.

Special thanks to Drs. Tad & Adriana James for their inspiration, support and encouragement.

To our families for their love, support and understanding.

To our friends, from many continents, for their friendship, discussions, wisdom, advice and inspiration.

To Emily Wu for her creative mind and for providing the illustrations, Carrie Merchant, Valeria Astorga, Angelo Mera, Teresa Ryan and Sue Gale for their brilliant proofreading and advice to improve the final draft.

To John Bannister for believing in this book and making it come true.

To all, we remain grateful always.

Marcia Becherel *M. D, Ph. D, Adv Dip. Naturopathy, Master Practitioner of NLP, Time Line Therapy™ and Hypnosis, Master NLP Coach*

Marcia holds a Medical Degree from Brazil with specialisation in Children's Health (Paediatrics) and a Ph. D in Microbiology and Public Health from Michigan State University, USA. In parallel with her medical and scientific career, Marcia has studied extensively Natural Therapies, Energy Medicine and Neurolinguistic Programming (NLP). Marcia is a Naturopath and a certified Master Practitioner of NLP, Time Line Therapy™ and Hypnosis that provides Wellness and Life Coaching.

Marcia's holistic approach to personal growth and self-empowerment integrates her medical expertise, scientific experience, knowledge of natural therapies, energy medicine, healthy lifestyle, and the cutting edge techniques of NLP for profound personal change to provide her clients with tailored solutions to quickly achieve optimum health, happiness and excellence.

Olivier J. Becherel *Ph. D, Master Practitioner of NLP, Time Line Therapy™ and Hypnosis, Master NLP Coach*

Olivier holds a Ph. D in Molecular Genetics & Biology from Louis Pasteur University, France. Olivier is a Senior Research Officer at the Queensland Institute of Medical Research in Brisbane, and his work focuses on elucidating the molecular and cellular aspects of neurodegeneration. Olivier is a certified Master Practitioner of NLP, Time Line Therapy™ and Hypnosis, and has ferocious curiosity and passion for the human mind and its unlimited potential. As an NLP Coach, Olivier aims at unleashing the power within individuals to help them achieve excellence and live a rich, joyful and meaningful life.

Emily Wu *Bc. D in Communication Design & Entrepreneurship*

Emily was a graduate of Queensland University of Technology and earned her Bachelor Degree in Communication Design and Entrepreneurship. She is now working with business associates in Brisbane and Sydney, specialising in leadership development. She chooses her career path in the design field in order to fully follow her heart and express her true self to the world.

Table of Contents

Foreword

Anxiety, the plague of the 21st century, consuming the energy and power of many people, can now be easily, rapidly and effortlessly tackled effectively in simplicity. In *Farewell to Anxiety: 7 Quick and Simple Steps to Rid yourself of Anxiety*, Marcia and Olivier share a series of tips that will enable you to understand *How* you *create* your own stress and anxiety, day in, day out. Following these simple steps, you will be able to quickly rid yourself of anxiety and stress by simply paying attention to your thoughts, and accepting that symptoms of anxiety and stress are *just* alerting you to the fact that you are out of balance. And that by simply, consciously directing your thoughts towards what you really want, you will easily restore homeostasis, inner peace and harmony. This little book is a quick and easy read that will provide you with practical, simple and rapid answers to overcoming anxiety and stress. You will also find within these lines, an overview of the physiological consequences of stress and anxiety and the amazing biological processes that have evolved to cope with it. Finally, Marcia and Olivier end this book by sharing an exquisite and powerful process, the Fast Anxiety Relief, based on Neurolinguistic Programming (NLP) and Time Line Therapy™ technologies. These are the most modern and cutting edge technologies for personal development and growth. Make sure you keep this book handy and you will be quickly and richly rewarded.

Drs. Tad & Adriana James,
Master Trainers of NLP and Time Line Therapy™

Introduction

Our modern society, with its many technological advances, forces us to do things quicker, better and faster, putting tremendous pressure on us. Not only do we have to do the right things, we also have to do them in the most perfect way in order to please.

With a constant focus on productivity, economy, and the ability to make money, modern lifestyle is taking an ever-increasing toll on our wellbeing, at physical, mental, emotional and/or spiritual levels.

As a consequence, human chronic conditions have flourished in the last 100 years, and amongst them, *Anxiety* and *Stress* have become two of the leading 'illnesses' of the 21th century.

It is our goal in *Farewell to Anxiety, 7 Quick and Simple steps to rid yourself of anxiety* to provide you with easy and simple steps to overcome anxiety by discovering the root cause and changing [*your*] world by shifting your focus.

We sincerely hope, with the help of this practical

handbook, that you will take the time to discover your true self, blast through limiting beliefs and negative emotions, and discover hidden potentialities, thus enabling you to experience a joyful and anxiety-free life.

Peace & Harmony,

Marcia & Olivier
Brisbane, 2009

"You can have anything you want in life
to the extent you pay attention.
If you fail to pay attention,
you'll pay it with pain."

Christopher Howard

Anxiety, clearly one of the most universal human experiences in the modern world, is what gives us panic attacks, makes our hands sweat, our hearts pound, gives us chills and creates knots in our stomach.

Anxiety seems to pop up at random, but as you will see later in this book, it only seems ... this way.

However, since many of us think it is random for the moment ... you never know when it will come back and thus everyone is anxious, aren't you? ...

PART 1

But what really is anxiety?

According to dictionary's definition, *anxiety* is a multisystem response to a *perceived* threat or danger. I insist on *perceived threat* or *perceived danger*. It reflects a combination of biochemical changes in the body, energy disturbances or blockages, personal history, memories, belief system, and of course the context of the social situation.

As far as we know, anxiety is a *uniquely human* experience.

Other animals clearly know fear, but human anxiety involves an ability, to use *memory* and *imagination* to move backward and forward in time, a skill that animals do not appear to have [*At least what most of us think for Now ... Who really knows!*]

A large portion of human anxiety is produced by the *anticipation of future events*.

In a nutshell,
"Anxiety is mainly the fear of the unknown."

Dr Spencer Johnson

Us and anxiety?

We, our being, is the combination of three qualities:

Mind [*conscious & unconscious*]

Body [*physical, biochemical, energetic*]

Spirit [*intangible, non-physical, energetic*]

And *we [You]* are a truly *magical, incredible* system that has the ability to *self-regenerate*.

[*Think about it, when we cut ourself, we heal our wound by ourselves. When we cut our hair off, it grows until we go to the hairdresser again.*]

Isn't it amazing!!

Our being's purpose is to keep US in *balance* [*at the mental, physical, energetic and spiritual levels*], no matter what is happening in our life.

Our body/mind/spirit's *prime function* is to keep us *healthy*. In other words, to keep us in an optimal physical, mental & spiritual health. Hence being in harmony with nature, thus simply being in *balance*.

The symptoms we experience when our body is trying to restore balance may not be pleasant, perhaps uncomfortable, may even be painful at times but they are not intended to hurt us.

[For example, if we are out of shape and not physically fit. The next time we do some exercise, our body will feel sore, tired, and we may even feel muscle pain. We have all experienced that. But it is not to hurt us, rather just to remind us that we need to exercise regularly to maintain a healthy and fit body.]

[Consider your body as a luxury car, the most expensive you can afford. You would certainly take good care, even extreme care of it, wouldn't you? Service it regularly, clean it, polish it ... and you would also know when to service it by just looking at the logbook. Finally you would also fill the tank with premium quality petrol.]

Well, similarly, anxiety is not a punishment but a *wake up call* from our being. It is the end result of years of accumulated ***physical***, ***emotional***, ***mental*** and ***spiritual stress***.

Anxiety is a *warning signal* to remind us that we are *out of balance*, and that it is time to do something to bring our being back in balance.

Since we are more than just a body obviously [*That's what you thought, right ...*], it is crucial to *integrate* our mental, energetic, emotional and spiritual components in the equation to run our body smoothly and harmoniously.

Anxiety reminds us that it is time to take care of ourselves ...

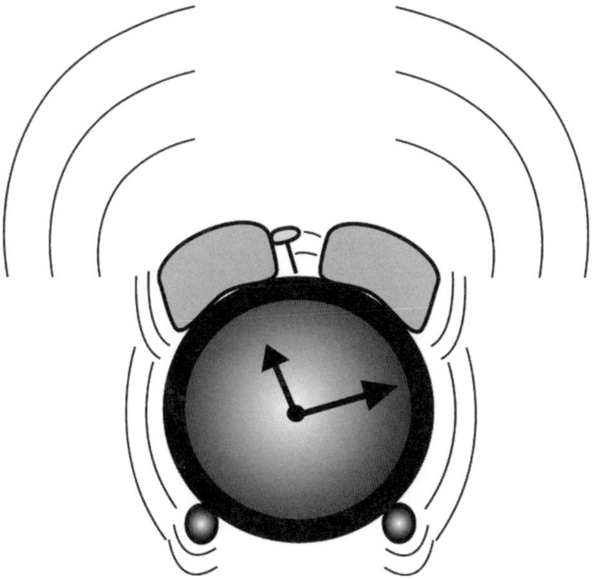

NOW!!

PART II

Step 1. How healthy are your mind, heart and spirit?

There are many reasons why you may have experienced anxiety, and I am sure that you know [*yours*] them very well, don't you? They most likely are different for everyone but nevertheless here are the most common ones:

- **Negativity** [*Pessimism, cynicism, criticism*]
- **Blame** [*Other people or yourself*]
- **Insecurity** [*Fear that something may happen to you/loved ones*]
- **Hurt** [*Yourself, someone else, your loved ones*]
- **Guilt** [*Of having made a mistake or done something wrong*]
- **Worry** [*About what will happen tomorrow, next week, next month, next year*]
- **Shame** [*Doing wrong things or a bad action*]

The more we *resist* being where we are, having what we're having, feeling what we're feeling, the more *pain* we add to our discomfort. And the more pain we feel.

"What you think about Expands. If your thoughts are focused on "Negative Emotions", then "Negative Emotions", by definition, will have to expand."

"We can't think about something we don't want to think about without thinking about it. Think about that ..."

❒ If you are physically burnt out, exhausted, and you get the flu [*by the way, this is usually how it happens*] you accept that you got the flu for a reason, don't you?

Whatever the reason might be!

And when you have the flu you accept its symptoms as being part of the deal. Well, you don't have much choice they are there ...

You then wait until the storm has gone, and if you are wise, and I know that you are deep inside, as we all are, you attend to those factors that made you vulnerable. Makes sense right? ❒

Accepting the experience of anxiety works in the same way

When we *accept* that we are anxious for a *reason*, and we also accept or at least *feel* the *symptoms* [*those described at the beginning and more* ...] that go with anxiety.

Similarly, you wait until the symptoms have passed and then you attend to those things that caused you to be anxious.

Similar to the flu, the symptoms that we feel are *physical, energetic, tangible [trust me, I know]*. But any threat or danger that we attach to those thoughts come from our *thinking*, our *imagination*.

It is all in our mind,
there is no actual danger!!
It is not the reality but our perception
of the situation!!

So next time you experience a dose of anxiety ...

- ✔ Let the symptoms *just be* the symptoms, not less, not more.
- ✔ Avoid adding to them with your thinking and imagination.
- ✔ Avoid judging people as you judge yourself as well.
- ✔ Expect to have these symptoms until you learn and understand more about what triggered them.
- ✔ Get curious and excited about the symptoms, be an astute observer, and notice them when they start to appear.
- ✔ Accept the experience of having these symptoms and learn from that experience.

for the Moment ...

"Have a mind that is opened to everything but attached to nothing."

Dr. Wayne Dyer

Step 2. (We are) in charge of our thinking, until proof of the contrary ...

Remember ...

"I think, therefore I am."

Rene Descartes

There is only one thing that makes us anxious and it is all in our head. That is our thinking, our inner chatter-box or self-talk. And remember that according to the Universal Law of Attraction:

We attract in our life
What we focus on

In other words, thinking of anxiety will bring more anxiety to our life. [*This is also valid for anything else and across context ...*]

Our thoughts determine our experience and our "reality"

Whether there is real danger or we are just thinking about the danger, it makes no difference as our body will react the same either way and develop the symptoms of anxiety.

As Dr. Richard Restak, neurologist and author of *The Naked Brain* tells us "*Thanks to our language and imaginative abilities, we humans don't always require a direct experience in order to be conditioned. The thinking about doing something activates the same brain regions that come into play when one actually does it.*" [*By the way, if you have the opportunity, I really recommend you read this book.*]

Let's play a little: *Have someone tell you this story and observe how you react.*

Why don't you close your eyes, take a deep breath, ignore your environment, relax, listen to your breath and focus on the voice of your friend who is telling you the story.

[... Imagine, you are in the Aussie bush, on a beautiful winter day ... that's right ... and you are getting tired after a long walk. You are ready to have a little rest under a nice gum tree, just a few steps ahead. Comfortably installed underneath, Ahh ... you are slowly finding your sleep. Suddenly you start to feel something moving, touching you, it's weird, but interesting, still keeping your eyes closed ... that's right, something is curling around your leg. Watch out it is a snake! ...]

I bet you probably opened your eyes straight away, even though you deliberately know that you are not in the bush and there is no snake ... Here is quick example of how your thinking [Listening to this little story relaxed, making mental images in your head and really imagining the scene vividly! can really give you a fright.]

Thus as beautifully said ...

"What seems to be, Is,
to those whom it seems to Be."

William Blake

You are the only one *in charge* of your thoughts, and that makes you the *most powerful* being. I, or somebody else can at best make an educated guess of what your thoughts are, but only you really know what is happening inside your mind.

We can *choose* our thoughts, and by the same token, we can *choose* to switch our anxious thoughts off in a split second. *Trust* me!

It all depends on US,
because We are the only One in control
of our thoughts

Because ... No one can slip Inside ... your Mind!

That's right! ...

To wipe out anxiety is as *simple* as that, turn around your thinking, and *change* your *focus*!

Here is HOW to do it ...

- **_Monitor_** yourself by being aware of your inner chatter-box (self-talk), or thinking.

- **_Challenge_** the thought and determine whether it is based on facts or if it is simply an illusion, a fantasy.

- **_Choose_** an alternative and change your thinking to support yourself. Open up to potentialities and focus on them.

- **_Interrupt_** the negative thinking pattern by leaving that thought alone and doing something else, thereby *interrupting* the negative thinking pattern.

As any exercise, may it be physical or mental, *mastery* takes *practice*, and as in any sport, *the more you practice, the better you become.*

Train your mind to detect negative thoughts when they *first* appear, and are still relatively easy to challenge, and *commit* to change your *thoughts* to support your being. *Be playful* about this training.

Anxiety is sneaky [*it is like a bad habit*]. It appears automatically without any warning. Detecting the first sign of anxiety and reacting immediately will deter it.

And when an anxious thought appears, *notice* it and *choose* a *healthy* alternative.

The more we become *aware* of our negative thoughts, the more we can *react quickly* and this will become a habit.

In the end, our anxiety will diminish and disappear for good

Step 3. Fire your anxiety radar

Anxiety is tricky, sneaky and may convince us that some of these things are essential and urgent.

But are they really ...?

Here is a quick list of thoughts that will definitely fire our anxiety radar

- ❒ Being a perfectionist and avoiding mistakes
- ❒ Predicting disasters
- ❒ Re-running the past
- ❒ Seeking approval from everybody
- ❒ Comparing ourselves to everybody
- ❒ Thinking that we are not good enough
- ❒ Feeling we are responsible for others' feelings
- ❒ Feeling that others control our feelings

ALL this is just an illusion
It is not real!!
It is our hallucination.
We created it ourselves

It is just a set of *limiting beliefs* that *nurture anxiety*. Limiting beliefs are beliefs that *inhibit* the *exploration* of a wider cognitive space that would otherwise be the case.

In other words, limiting beliefs are *boxing you in the boundaries of your thinking*. It's like being a bird in a cage. Except that this time it is a virtual imaginary cage, it doesn't exist, it's purely in our head.

These may be strongly held *unconscious beliefs*, and are often tied in with *self-image* or *perceptions* about the world.

These limiting beliefs may have come from our childhood, upbringing, our family, our friends, education, interpersonal relationships, religion, and so on ...

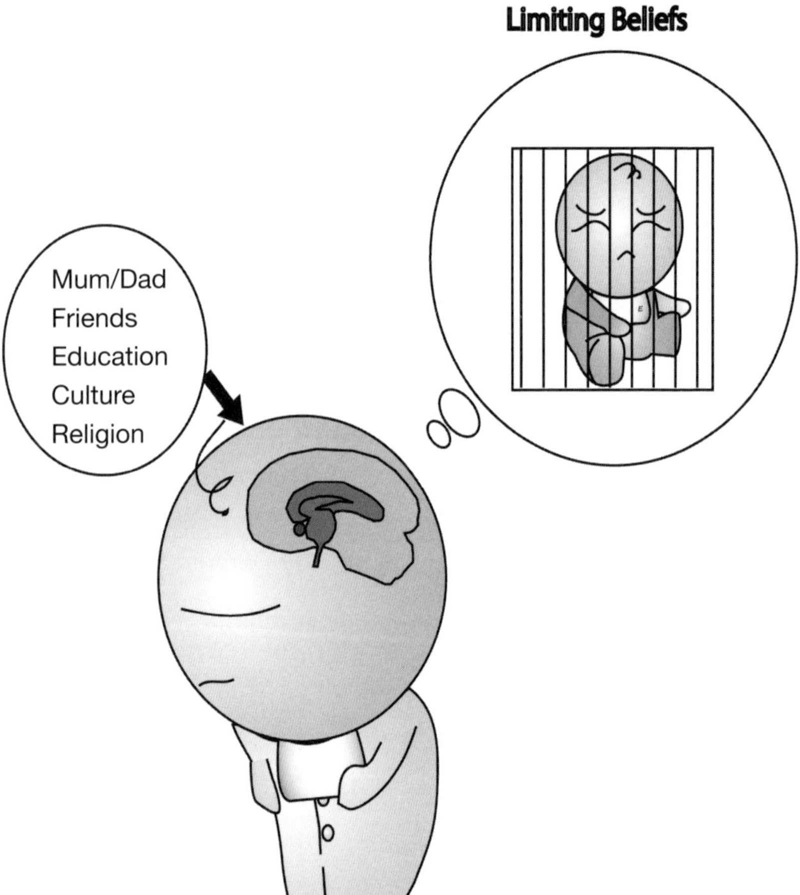
Limiting Beliefs
Mum/Dad
Friends
Education
Culture
Religion
Emi

And all these limiting beliefs are based on a *single negative emotion*: ***FEAR***.

- ❐ Fear of being judged
- ❐ Fear of being unworthy
- ❐ Fear of disapproval
- ❐ Fear of not belonging
- ❐ Fear of being vulnerable
- ❐ Fear of being rejected
- ❐ Fear of doing something wrong
- ❐ Fear of not being loved
- ❐ Fear of fears

So let's take a deep breath,
Humm ...... Ahh ......
and think about ...

- ❑ **What would happen if we didn't fear these things?**
- ❑ **What would happen if we could get rid of our anxiety?**

Remember, if we want to get rid of our anxiety, thinking about it is not the solution as it only feeds it. That was just a reminder to make sure that you were paying attention ...

We are and will become what we think about all day

"You create your thoughts, your thoughts create your intention, and your intention creates your reality."

Dr. Wayne Dyer

But...

- ❑ **Is it possible that our anxiety wants to give us a message, that anxiety could have a purpose?**

Yes, that's right!

Anxiety is just a warning signal to tell us a simple thing. And you know what it is, don't you ...

We need to do things differently!
It is that simple!

If we are willing to *listen* (instead of escaping), anxiety may *guide* us and let us *understand* what we *really* need to do *differently*.

Consider anxiety as a little red flag [like the one in your e-mail program when you get an important message and that you need to address promptly] that will pop up *everytime, not at random*, but *only* when we are *out of balance*.

*When we feel and experience fear,
anxiety is actually telling us
to slow down, breathe and analyse
the situation*

*Consider anxiety as your
personal internal alarm system
towards negative emotions
and limiting beliefs*

Anxiety is warning that we are ...

- Trying to seek approval from others.

- Being inflexible with ourselves or others.

- Not being in the present moment, but living in the future, or who knows when ... or where.

- Not being ourselves, but pretending to be.

- Paying too much attention to other's opinions and not listening to our intuition, our truth.

- Devaluating ourselves by lowering our self-esteem.

*Anxiety alerts us to
what needs rebalancing in our life*

Step 4. Change your thoughts change your life ...

Experience, accept and *learn* from your anxiety to improve your *Now*, your moment of *Power*, and your future.

What is behind anxiety?

Anxiety reveals a *hidden* part of us either conscious or unconscious, our *limiting beliefs*.

For example:

- ❑ Life is a constant struggle.
- ❑ I need to struggle to succeed.
- ❑ If I give Love, I will get hurt.
- ❑ I am not good enough to succeed.
- ❑ I must keep people happy, even if I have to pretend.
- ❑ I must not express my feelings. It's a sign of weakness.
- ❑ I can't be powerful. It's scary and hard.
- ❑ Only dishonest people make money.
- ❑ I am helpless.
- ❑ I am worthless.
- ❑ Everything must be perfect and I have to control everything.
- ❑ It is not OK to loose control.

Most of this comes from our *childhood experiences*, our *upbringing*, our *education*, our *environment*, our *culture*, and the *social hypnosis*.

Our education, our experiences, our relationships, our environment *define who* we are. But take away our thoughts, and we could be any one of a million different people.

Our thoughts are the essence of our entire life. *Wrong thoughts cripple our existence. Right thoughts can change our life and turn it around in the blink of an eye.*

"No-one gives you your personality,
not even your family or your culture,
YOU just create it yourself."

"You are today where your thoughts have
brought you; you will be tomorrow
where your thoughts take you."

James Allen

It is during our childhood that we *learn beliefs*, and thus at the same time *limiting beliefs* and acquire *emotions* (either good or bad):

- How love functions
- How powerful people behave and act
- That expressing our feelings can be wrong
- And that our behaviour affects others

However, children are in the *learning stage* and therefore have only a *limited experience*, they don't see the big picture, and therefore take things *literally* and *personally*. This mostly happens *unconsciously* and by definition, most of the time we are not aware of it.

The *only* thing that a child [*by the way, adults too!*] wants is *love*, all day, every day, and unconditionally.

Children will develop strategies to attract attention and love, *but* day after day, month after month, year after year, we *all learn* that some parts of ourselves are not OK because those parts aren't loved as much as other parts.

"The person identifies more basically and intimately with just a facet of his total organism, and this facet, which he feels to be his real self, is known as the ego, the personality."

Ken Wilber

Step 5. How to restore balance

If we realise that our anxiety is only telling us what brings us out of balance, it will also help us understand how to get back in balance.

Here are some very simple steps that will bring us back in balance & harmony

1. *Pay attention* to and *analyse* the *warning signs*, they will *reveal* what our REAL fear is.

2. *Learn* from our *experience* and our *past* to *design* a plan for the future.

3. *Monitor* our *thinking* and our *habits* to prevent a new surge.

4. *Change* our *thoughts* and *focus* to seek alternative routes.

5. *Realise* that our *true self* is a *being of light* and *love* ourselves for what we are, not what we pretend we are or want to be.

6. Remember that we are *always* doing *the best we can* at any moment with the resources we have.

7. We *are in control* and the only one *responsible* for our thoughts.

8. There is *no failure*, but only *feedback* and results [*either that you do like or don't*]

9. It is not our fault, *forgive ourselves*.

Love yourself,
be gentle with yourself,
and believe in yourself

Loving ourselves is our first
necessary step towards
overcoming anxiety

We *first* need to *accept* and *love* ourselves, before expecting that others will like us.

Why? Do you know the answer, think about it for a moment ... Well, here is the answer!

We only *perceive* what we *project* out in the world. And therefore, if you project low self-esteem or that you don't love or accept yourself for what you truly are, don't be surprised if you receive the same.

By healing our relationship with ourselves, we will heal our relationship with others

Do not listen to naysayers or people that always criticise you, remember that you are the captain in charge of your ship.

We *decide* what we want to *believe* and we are the only one that really knows US.

"If you don't design your own life plan, chances are you'll fall into someone else's plan. And guess what they have planned for you ... Not much."

Jim Rohn

We are responsible for ourselves,
our wellbeing, our well-thinking,
Not for the life of others

Whatever opinion others may hold of us, it is up to us to *decide* whether to *believe* them or *not*, we can disagree, nobody can force us to accept their views.

We are in charge of our thinking.
This makes us the
most powerful being.
Whatever we do it is perfect
as we are a being of light.

Accept *ALL* the *parts* of yourself and stop apologising for being yourself.

Take charge of yourself, be your own captain, your own motivation team, your own counsellor, your own best coach, your best friend, and loose the "disease to please everyone".

This is all good and nice in a wonderful world ... but if someone hurts us terribly.

Well, consider our two options ...

1] **Remain wounded and live in and suffer from the past – or more accurately, suffer from the *illusion* of the past.**

Since the past is in our head [our mind and memories], we can't touch it, we can't grasp it, we can't get hold of it, it is intangible, it doesn't exist! It's a construction [*ours*] of our thinking and imagination.

Only the present moment, the *NOW*, exists.

2] Disconnect from the power of the past, - the power of the illusion of the past - and come back in the present moment, in the NOW and choose how we want to live in the NOW.

Unplug yourself [*click...*] from that mental, energetic and emotional hallucination that drains your energy and cripples your existence.

After all, being successful and living an exciting life isn't it what we all want?

Step 6. Cruise control on anxiety-free life

How about if we could live a life where there was less to be upset, angry or worried about?

Would our anxiety really diminish?

❒ *Would you like it?*

Most human misery comes from our beliefs – actually in this case our *limiting beliefs* - what we are convinced of, or what others have convinced us of:

- ❑ Not accepting things as they are
- ❑ Not living in the present moment, the NOW
- ❑ Resisting change
- ❑ Remaining and willing to be stuck in pain
- ❑ Giving away our personal power
- ❑ Being on the effect side, looking for reasons and excuses, and not at cause (responsibility) for what happens to us.

Let's have a quick look at these illusory [self-created] problems ...

➲ **<u>Not accepting things as they are</u>**

- ***What if we could find novel opportunities to any situation?***

- ***What if we could learn from the situation?***

- ***What if we had fewer expectations and were more flexible?***

- ***What if we could increase our tolerance towards others?***

➲ **<u>Not living in the present</u>**

- ***What if we shut down our inner chatter-box for a moment and stopped living in the future and predicting what could happen?***

- ***What if we also stop living in the past and regretting what happened?***

- ***What if we just decide to focus and live in the Now, our only true real moment of power?***

➲ **Resisting change**

Nature is constantly changing, this is an observable fact. Everybody agrees on it and everybody experiences it.

By paying attention to nature we will quickly realise that *everything is changing* and *nothing stays the same*.

- ***What if we plan for change to follow nature's way, instead of being stuck in an artificial and unnatural permanence?***
- ***What if we could realise that even tough times are only there temporarily, and they will inevitably move way, as everything changes in life?***

And that soon enough, good times will come back again.

Thus, instead of focusing on these bad times, choose to focus on the good times

➲ Remaining and willing to be stuck in pain

- ***What if we realise that pain is only a warning sign and that it is time to sort some things out?***
- ***What if we could use pain to remind ourselves to make some improvements in our life?***
- ***What if we used the experience of pain to learn from it and transform a negative attitude towards a positive one?***

"When we are no longer able to change a situation, we are challenged to change ourselves."

Viktor Frankl

➲ Giving away your personal power

- ***What if we give ourselves all the things we hope that others will give us?***
- ***What if we decide to like ourselves Right Here, Right Now, instead of waiting for others to tell us?***
- ***What if we realise that we are the only one in charge and that no-one can hurt us, let us down or even betray us if we don't give them the power to do so?***

"The one thing you can't take away from me is the way I choose to respond to what you do to me. The last of one's freedoms is to choose ones attitude in any given circumstance."

Viktor Frankl

➲ Be on the effect side and not at cause with what happens to you

- ***What if we don't judge life as either fair or unfair, but as a natural unfolding process?***

- ***What if we decide to be at cause for whatever comes to our life?***

- ***What if we decide that we are the only one responsible for our life and we can change it if we wish to do so?***

- ***What if we realise that we only perceive out there what we are, and that our perception is purely a reflection of ourself?***

- ***What if we understand that by changing our thoughts, we would actually change our life?***

- ***What if we discover that our life is boxed in by the boundaries of our thinking, and that the potential of our life exists in this Universe of infinite possibilities?***

"There are two primary choices in life: to accept conditions as they exist, or to accept the responsibility for changing them."

Denis Waitley

"You will see it, when you believe it."

Dr. Wayne Dyer

Step 7. Coming next, moving beyond your (imaginary) boundaries

Life may sometimes appears as a rough and bumpy ride, but the more we focus on what we want, and we commit and act towards our vision, the journey will become smoother than we can imagine.

True for any journey, whether in our life, or while going on holidays; without a clear vision, we will end up lost along our way.

So remember, our road map indicates everything, we just need to *pay attention*.

"When you travel towards your objective, be sure to pay attention to the path. The path teaches us the best way to arrive and enriches us while we are travelling along it."

Paulo Coelho

To embark on this journey you were given a vehicle, which is composed of your Body, Mind and Spirit [*personality*].

This vehicle is yours for life, and it is your ***responsibility*** to ***nurture*** and ***take care*** of it. It may not seem right at times, but it is only a matter of making the necessary adjustments.

[Think of your car, you need to tune it, to service it, to clean it, to put the right fuel in it, from time to time to make it function properly and reach your destination.]

We may find some hitchhikers along the path, some will be fun, some won't be, some we wish we didn't meet, but they will undoubtedly help us to discover ourselves. And it is up to us to learn from these encounters.

While some will help us, others will distract us from the path or push us in the wrong direction, but remember that we are the driver and therefore we are always in charge of our vehicle.

We may make a few wrong turns, who else never did, hit a few obstacles, we may temporarily stall, end up carrying too much baggage, or we may just cruise along.

In each case, we will have learned valuable experiences and learn how to follow our path.

Remember, it is our journey, and we are the only driver that can steer it wherever we like and with whomever we want.

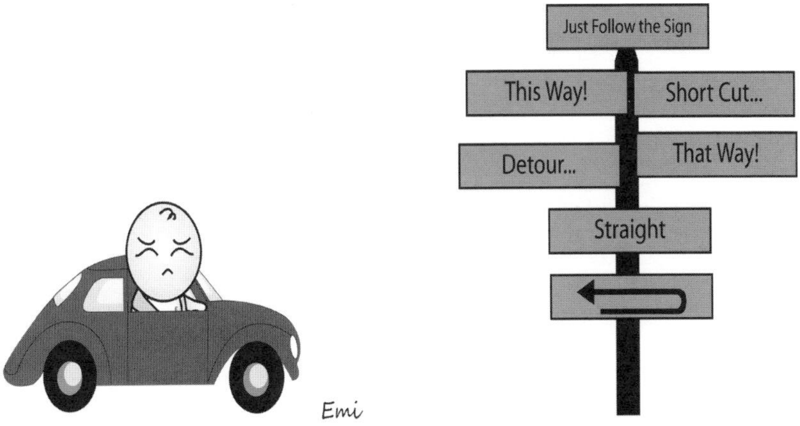

In a Nutshell

- ✔ *Anxiety is mainly fear of the future*
- ✔ *It is all in our mind, it isn't real!*
- ✔ *Anxiety is our personal Alarm System that tells us that WE are out of balance!*
- ✔ *Anxiety reminds US that it is time to take care of ourselves and do something differently!*
- ✔ *Accept the experience of anxiety, be curious, learn from it, but do NOT stay attached to it*
- ✔ *Our thoughts determine our experience and our reality ...*
- ✔ *We attract in our life what WE focus on all day, therefore think carefully of what You want!*
- ✔ *It all depends on US because WE are the only one in control of our thoughts!*
- ✔ *Remember, change your thoughts, change your reality, and therefore YOU will change your life!*

PART III

The Biology of Stress and Anxiety: From Biology to Energy to thoughts

We live in a very stressed out society. Everybody will agree with that. That is why stress has become one of the major epidemics of the Modern society. Stress and anxiety [*a form of stress*] affects our health [*physical, mental, emotional and spiritual*] and our behaviour.

So let us consider that we, humans, react to environmental stimuli through our *perception* of the outside world and *elicit* appropriate *behavioural responses*.

This is in fact the emerging current view of scientific research since genetic defects account for about 5% of the population. The other 95% that are genetically healthy still experience diseases.

How we react to our environment, or how we think in response to some past or future moment that may be stressful, is responsible for most of the maladies, both physical and emotional, from which we suffer.

Stress is when our body *moves out* of normal *homeostatic balance*. When we react to something, the body produces numerous chemical changes that alter the normal psychological-chemical inner order.

The stress response is what the body does to re-establish normal homeostatic balance

When we *repeatedly* place ourselves in a *high-stress mode*, or when we are *hyper–vigilant* in looking for/or thinking about [*anxiety*] *stressors* that may affect us in some future moment, we engage the body's emergency response to stress.

Given that our body is composed of a community of 50-70 trillion cells, our *perception* thus controls cell behaviour.

In addition, we all know that our *centre of command* is our *Brain* and *Nervous System*, in other words the

Mind. So rather than behaving as programmed genetic automatons [*Hey, we are not robots* ...], *biological behaviour* is *dynamically* linked to the *environment* through its interpretation (*perception*) made by our *Mind*.

Stress and Performance

Stress is not all bad. A *minimum amount* of stress is required to keep us *alert* and help us going forward. This is where an *appropriate* amount of stress will create a *healthy tension* which will help us in reaching our *peak performance* (Figure 1).

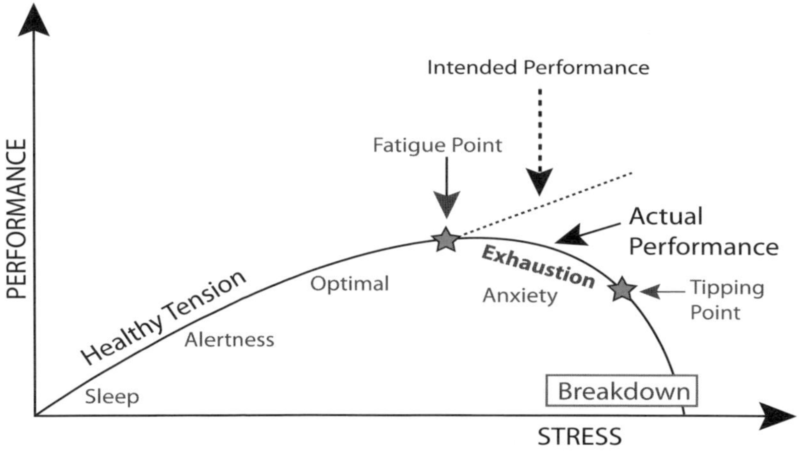

Figure 1. Stress vs Performance

However, stress becomes toxic when we reach the *fatigue point*. Instead of continuously increasing our performance [*as we would like or think it will*], we soon reach *exhaustion*, where most of our energy stores are depleted and we cannot replenish our stock, and from then onwards, it is all downhill!

By being continually on emergency mode, our body doesn't have the time or the resources necessary to repair or regenerate itself.

We then reach a *Tipping point* where the slightest minimal arousal may precipitate a total breakdown, energetic, physical, mental, emotional and spiritual.

This breakdown is also known as illness, injury or overload ...

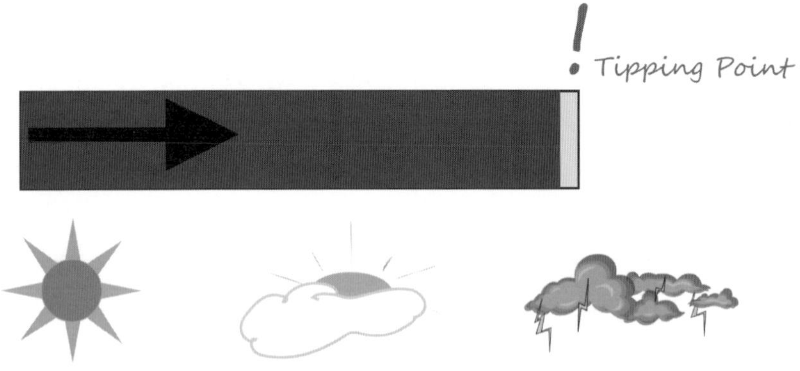

What happens at the Cellular level?

There are two major ways our cells can respond to the environment. This is not only true for humans, but also for any living organism.

They can either be in **Growth** or in **Protection/ Survival Mode.**

For example, when we perceive that the environment is safe and supportive, our Mind signals to our cells that it is time to grow, expand and maintain the body in balance for optimum performance.

In contrast, stressful situations send different messages to our cells, telling them to adopt a defensive protective/survival attitude.

So, Stress [*which by the way is only a perception, as we mentioned earlier*] puts us on living in the emergency or protection mode and as a consequence of being energetically drained, protection systems rob the growth systems.

This is because it takes energy to be in growth mode but it takes even more energy to be in protection/

survival mode.

Thus, if the majority of our body cells are in protection/ survival mode, they will consume the energy and steal it away from growth processes, resulting in our body being in default of energy and beginning to degenerate and fall into disease and dysfunction.

While our cells are either in growth or in protection, our body [*a cell community*] can be in a range of being in growth and protection with many variables (Figure 2).

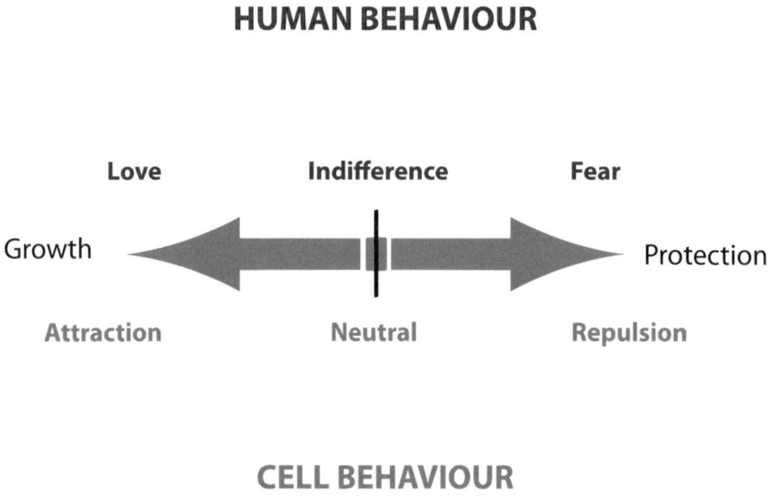

Figure 2. Human behaviour ⇔ Cell behaviour

Biological response to Love vs Fear

The body deals with growth and protection using two systems:

1. The *Visceral system* is the overriding system during growth. It provides the *metabolic support* and is comprised of Respiration, Digestion, Excretion, Reproduction and Internal protection (Immune system).

2. The *Somatic system* is the overriding system during protection. It provides *physical support* and is comprised of Musculoskeletal, Connective Tissue and External protection (Skin).

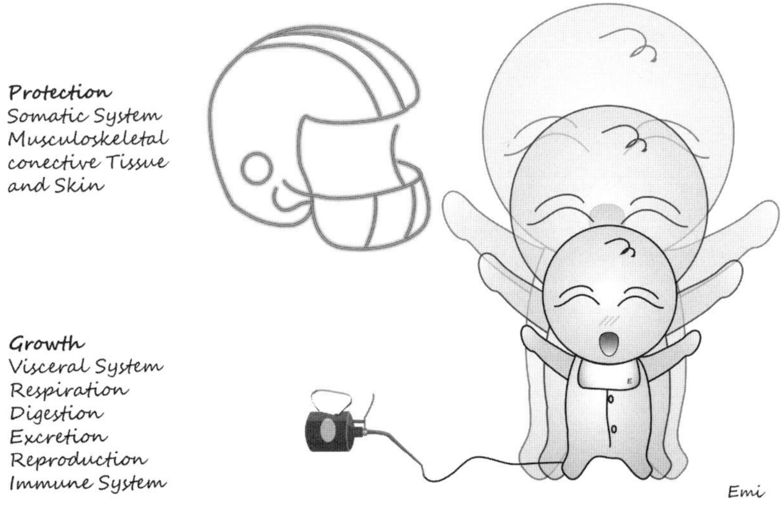

Biology of the stress response

We, our body, respond to stress *via* two pathways:

The *Neurological response* and the *Chemical response*.

The neurological response is immediate. The *autonomic nervous system* (ANS) turns on in response to *something real or imagined* in our environment [*remember that anxiety is a perceived threat or danger*]. It then passes the information to the *adrenal system*, the *Master switch* in the body that switches between the growth (Visceral) and protection/survival (Somatic) modes.

In the growth mode, the visceral system is in charge. When a threat is perceived, the adrenal system sends a protection signal which activates the somatic system, and the body goes into the protection/survival mode.

In the protection/survival mode, blood flow is squeezed out of the viscera and is channelled to the muscles and skeletal system. In addition the blood flow is suppressed in the forebrain and routed to the hindbrain stem where the *Fight – or – Flight* response kicks in.

The body shuts down or limits nonessential functions and we end up in a state of heightened awareness and energy, ready to fight *or* flight.

Intelligence goes down as far as calm and rational thinking is concerned, and reactive, instinctive processes take the command. We *unconsciously react* instead of consciously planning our actions.

If you have ever felt unable to think, brain fogged or uneasy with knots in your stomach, you just moved into the protection/survival mode.

The H-P-A Axis

Similarly to the neurological response, the chemical response can be *triggered* by a mere *internal thought* as well as a reaction to our *environment*.

Under stress, the *brain* fires diverse neural networks which send a signal to the *hypothalamus* that will then signal to our cells to produce the appropriate behaviour in response to the signal (Figure 3).

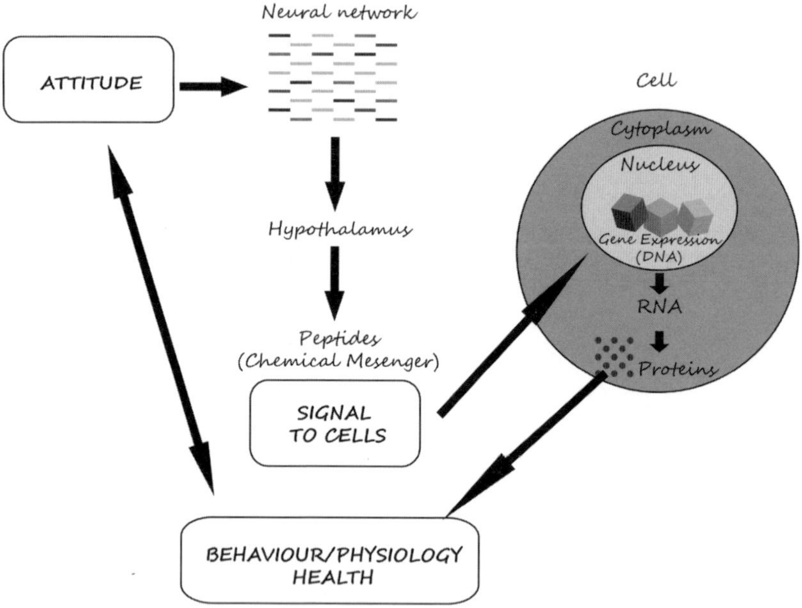

Figure 3. The Chemical Response

In the stress response, a *chemical messenger*, corticotrophin releasing hormone (**CRH**) is released from the *hypothalamus* to signal to the *pituitary gland* (*Master gland*). When the pituitary gets the signal, it relays the signal by making a secondary messenger, adrenocorticotropic hormone (**ACTH**) that goes to the *adrenal glands* that in turn secretes adrenal hormones (glucocorticoids, **cortisol** and **adrenalin**) which ultimately change the internal order of the body (Figure 4).

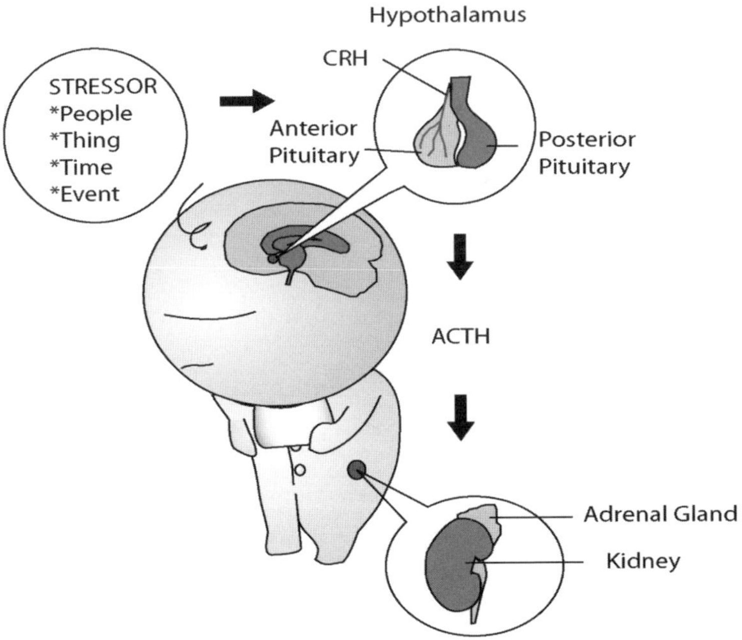

Figure 4. The Hypothalamus-Pituitary-Adrenal axis

Effects of the Chemical response

The chemical response results in the constriction of blood vessels in the viscera causing more blood to go the extremities (arm and legs) to be ready in case of *Fight - or - Flight* response.

The adrenal glands also send out *glucocorticoids* to trigger the *Fight - or - Flight* response. High levels of cortisol damage the immune system, shutting it down to save energy that will be available to serve the stress situation. Thus, when we are involved in a stress reaction, the body systems responsible for repair and regeneration are compromised.

The Fight - or - Flight response is all about mobilising energy for immediate action

If there is a real and immediate stress signal, this is the natural and preferred state of reaction of the body. The same applies if a threat is perceived, whether it is real or just imagined.

Problems arise when we are repeatedly (chronically) stressed because our growth systems and immune systems are constricted or shut down.

This is why we experience more sickness during periods of high stress, loose our intelligence, and react automatically or instinctively. If we are repetitively under stress, it will take us much longer to heal, because that process isn't a high priority item.

We can suffer from immune-mediated diseases like allergies, infectious influenza, etc. The reproductive processes such as ovulation and sperm production are also affected by stress. Impotence, infertility and miscarriage are all common side effects of chronic stress.

The more stress in our life, the more frequently we get sick, and the effects of a compromised immune system show up in many forms. If the hypothalamus-pituitary-adrenal axis is hyperactive, cells in the body may stop taking up glucose in response to insulin, and diabetes may result.

Chronic stress increases our blood sugar levels by altering the activity of the pancreas, the liver, and the storage mechanism in fat cells, and is also responsible for many aches and pains that we experience. Excess CRH plays a role in mental disorders, and contributes to phobias and panic attacks.

When we are living in protection mode, our brain becomes attuned to function as radar, sweeping the environment. When a threat is perceived, we are instantly on alert, and we moved into a state of heightened anticipation [*sometimes over expectation*] that something potentially harmful could [*or will*] happen.

When we anticipate being in the presence of a stressful situation, we experience stress symptoms

All the changes in our internal chemical balance will always react in response to that stress by releasing high amounts of adrenaline and glucocorticoid triggering all the changes in the chemical balance in the body.

Chronic stress, the repeated process of keeping the stress response activated all the time, is what really does the damage.

Our bodies are not designed for long-term stress

When the stress response is constantly activated, we are headed for disease. Cells in permanent stress will either die or go into disorganisation, and the [cellular] community will fall apart, leading to the apparition of cancer and other illnesses.

The Cell's response to chronic stress

Cells in a community can adopt three responses to extended period stress:

1. Shrink and die.

2. Excrete things out of their immediate environment in an attempt to reduce the stress [*high energy consumption*], which is not sustainable over long period of time. They try to adapt their environment to them.

3. They can adapt to the conditions of their environment, change the expression of their genes, their biology to accomodate with the stressful environment.

What should I do?

Stress is *unavoidable*. The key is to *limit* the kind of stress we experience to acute stress, which is much less harmful to the body than chronic stress. The more times we activate the stress response, the more difficult it becomes to turn it off.

We, humans, are subjected to three categories of stress: physical, chemical, and emotional or psychological. When we are exposed to any of these three categories, the body will respond to each type in the exact same manner, as with an automatic reaction.

Specific stresses affect *different* parts or organs of the body. As we said before, symptoms are just trying to tell you that you are not running your body in a coordinated and harmonious fashion.

Emotional/psychological stressors are just as potentially threatening to our survival as are physical ones. The non-physical threats we face are more complex and can't be handled with the Fight - or - Flight response.

We, humans, suffer the greatest damage from emotional/psychological stress.

Due to our complex interaction with the environment, emotional/psychological stress is much more *prevalent* in our modern world. It produces physical stress, which subsequently produces a chemical stress. That chemical stress, in turn, produces an ongoing physical stress, which then creates a physical pain and thus produces a psychological stress, thereby creating a full circle ...

Thus by *understanding* what the *emotions* are that elicit each stress, you will be able to deal more effectively with the stress and thus *relieve* your body and *switch* from the protection mode into the growth mode.

By taking a closer look at our *beliefs* and *thought patterns*, we can begin to notice what kinds of *filters* we are wearing that *colour* our *perception* of reality.

"There is everything in the world, both love and fear, but if we focus on fear we draw those things to us because that is all the filters will let through. If we focus on love, we draw growth to us because that is what the filters will allow through."

Dr. Bruce Lipton

We are all infinitely more powerful than we have allowed ourselves to know [believe]

If you don't like the way your life is going, change your beliefs ...

Pay attention to your thoughts and analyse them

The Secret to a Magical Life is to watch our thoughts

PART IV

Fast Anxiety Relief Technique

Now that we've covered some of the *reasons* from which you may experience anxiety and stress, and you've seen how *harmful chronic stress* and *anxiety* can be on your body, it is time for us to share with you a powerful technique that will help you overcome your anxiety in the blink of an eye.

The *Fast Anxiety Relief* technique was developed by Drs Tad & Adriana James (Master Trainers of Neurolinguistic Programming or NLP), and is based on Time Line Therapy™. (The *Fast Anxiety Relief* technique is shown here with the permission of Drs. Tad & Adriana James. - Copyright 1987-2008, Drs. Tad & Adriana James and The Tad James Co., LLC.)

Remember that, as we mentioned before, *anxiety is mostly the fear of the future.*

What is Time Line Therapy™?

Time Line Therapy™ is a technique which takes advantage of *active imagination* to create immediate, positive and powerful changes.

As Albert Einstein said:

"Imagination is more important than knowledge."

Time Line Therapy™ can assist you to overcome mental obstacles [*limiting decisions, limiting beliefs, negative emotions*] that prevent you from being, doing and/or having what you really, really, really want.

Everything, we experience or notice in the world is *encoded* in our mind, and we can recall it because it is *associated* with *time*.

For example, we remember when we were younger, our first day of school, our first date, got our first car, or when we got married, etc ...

All these *memories* are *organised* inside ourselves unconsciously and *linked* to the *notion of time* which ultimately *determines* our *emotional* state and *behaviours*.

Our *personality* is a mere *collection of memories*, and everyone has their own *personal perception of time*, which is mostly *spatial* in nature. It is this *perception of time* that makes Time Line Therapy™ so *powerful* and *effective*.

Finally, we should mention that *there is no inherent meaning in any event, situation or occurrence other than that which we attach to it*.

So as we said before, if you don't like what you are, do, or have, change is only one thought away.

We hope that you will find this technique helpful and use it as much as you want. Don't be afraid to get addicted to it, or pay it forward. Please feel free to share it with your loved ones, friends, and colleagues.

Are you ready for it NOW??

Now as we said, all your memories, all your personality, all that defines you, is linked to the notion of time.

So before starting the process, you need to get in touch with your *Time Line*. Don't worry, this is very easy and doesn't hurt!

Here we go...

"If I were to ask your unconscious mind, where your past is, to which direction would you point?"

"And your future, what direction would you point if I asked your unconscious mind, where is your future?"

Here it is not your conscious concept of where your past/future is, that is important, but rather your *unconscious*. Remember it is *active imagination!*

"Notice that you can draw a line that joins your past and your future!"

Good! This is your Time Line ... easy enough!

Now that you are aware of your Time Line, here is the process ...

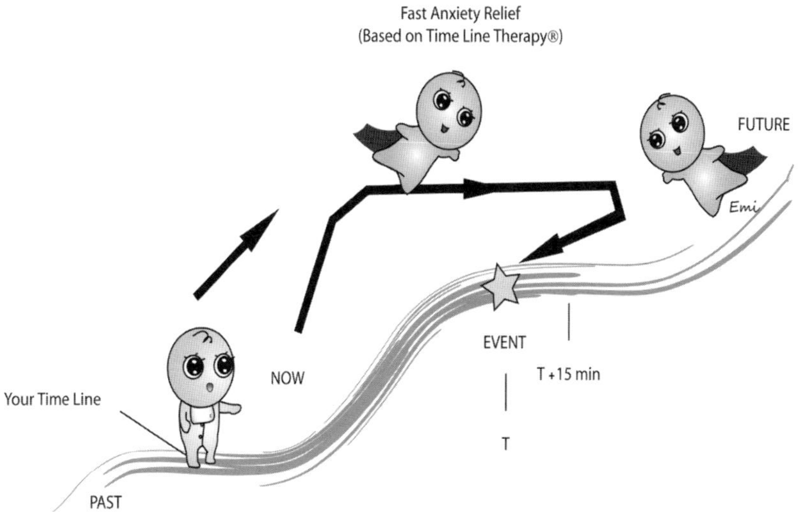

1. Ask yourself **what** you are anxious about, be really **clear** and **specific**. [*This is very important for the success of the process*].

2. Now, *imagine* you are rising above your Time Line, just floating up above it ...

3. *Float above* your Time Line into the future, **15 minutes** past the *successful completion* of that event (T) about which you were anxious.

4. And when you're there, *turn* and *look towards Now*, along your Time Line.

5. *Now*, where is your anxiety? . . . [*Yes, it's Gone!*]

6. *Come back* into **Now**.

If you would like, you may want to check if it is really gone.

Yes! I think you want to check ...

[*If I were you I would definitely check!*]

So, just think about what used to make you anxious, and notice if there is no anxiety.

And you will find ... to your surprise ...

[*I know pretty weird, but pretty cool*]

- -- -- -- -- -- *Yep, It's Gone* -- -- -- -- --

Notes:

You may choose to keep your eyes open, or close them, as you prefer, do what works best for you.

If the anxiety is still there, are you really imagining the ***successful completion*** of the event?

➲ Now go back to step #3.

Sometimes, you may have to go further into the future [*i.e. 1 hour, several hours, 1 day, a few days …*] after the ***successful completion*** of that event.

All this is fine, you just need to experience it, feel it, and find out what works best for you.

Be playful about it!

References & Further reading ...

Paulo Coelho. *Life, Selected Quotations.* HaperCollins Publishers. 2007.

Joe Dispenza. D.C. *Evolve Your Brain. The Science of Changing your Mind.* Health Communications, Inc. 2007.

Dr. Wayne Dyer. *Being in Balance: Nine principles for Creating Habits to Match your Desires.* Hay House Inc. 2006.

Dr. Richard Restak. *The Naked Brain.* Harmony Books. 2006.

Dr. Candace Pert. *Molecules of Emotions, The Science behind Mind-Body Medicine. Scriber.* 1997.

Dr. Tad James & Wyatt Woodmall. *Time Line Therapy™ and the Basis of Personality.* Meta Publications. 1988.

Dr. Spencer Johnson. *One Minute for Myself, A Small Investment, A Big Reward.* Published by W. Morrow, 1985.

Dr. Spencer Johnson. *Peaks and Valleys, Making Good Times And Bad Times Work For You - At Work And In Life.* ATRIA Books, 2009.

Afterword

We hope that you enjoyed reading *Farewell to Anxiety, 7 Quick and Simple steps to rid yourself of anxiety* as much as we enjoyed writing it.

And remember ...

Our focus determines the world we live in,
and by shifting our focus towards
what we want in life the Universe will
conspire to deliver what we ask for.

There is no failure,
only results and feedback.
And if you don't like the results,
it's up to you to change.

Finally,
the only moment of power is NOW.
So Do it Right NOW!

Emi

until next time ...

Have Wonderful Day
and feeling Great for
No good reason!!

Hungry for more practical tips? Want a step-by-step guide?

Exclusive to *'Farewell to Anxiety'* Readers & Friends, Marcia and I have put together an *ACTION* Book to guide you through the process of letting go of anxiety and start living a rich and stress-free life.

'Farewell to Anxiety, The ACTION Book' is finally available after tons of requests.

'Farewell to Anxiety, The ACTION Book' guides you through *step-by-step* to *FAST TRACK* your way into a life FREE from anxiety, stress and help you bring Balance and Harmony, *In and Out*.

As a new Friend of our Tribe, visit ...
www.freefromanxietyandstress.com to request your **FREE COPY** of *'Farewell to Anxiety, The ACTION Book'* (Valued at $27.00) and start enjoying the results **RIGHT NOW!**

Coming NEXT:

- The FAST ANXIETY RELIEF Audio Program
- And many more to come!

Make sure to add to your bookmarks
www.freefromanxietyandstress.com and *stay tuned*
for more to come ...

WANT MORE ???

OK, OK ... we knew that would happen!

Join our Tribe and get **mouth-watering** tips on *HOW to TRANSFORM your life* and reap the benefits with our **UNIQUE Monthly Newsletter** - *'Free Yourself & Start Living'*.

You get *SPECIAL, PROVEN, POWERFUL* and *ACTION-ABLE* Strategies, Tips, and *WISDOM* on how to *Free Yourself and Start Living* the life you deserve.

Stop sitting on the fence, and make the ***best decision*** of your life **RIGHT NOW!**

Join our Tribe **NOW** and *Free Yourself and Start Living.*

To subscribe to *Free Yourself and Start Living,*
contact us at:

newsletter@freefromanxietyandstress.com

For a Personal Breakthrough

Marcia & Olivier provide *UNIQUE*

Life & Wellness Coaching

that will guide you through and support your

Transformational Journey and Evolution.

Please contact us at:

coaching@freefromanxietyandstress.com